to Mamma

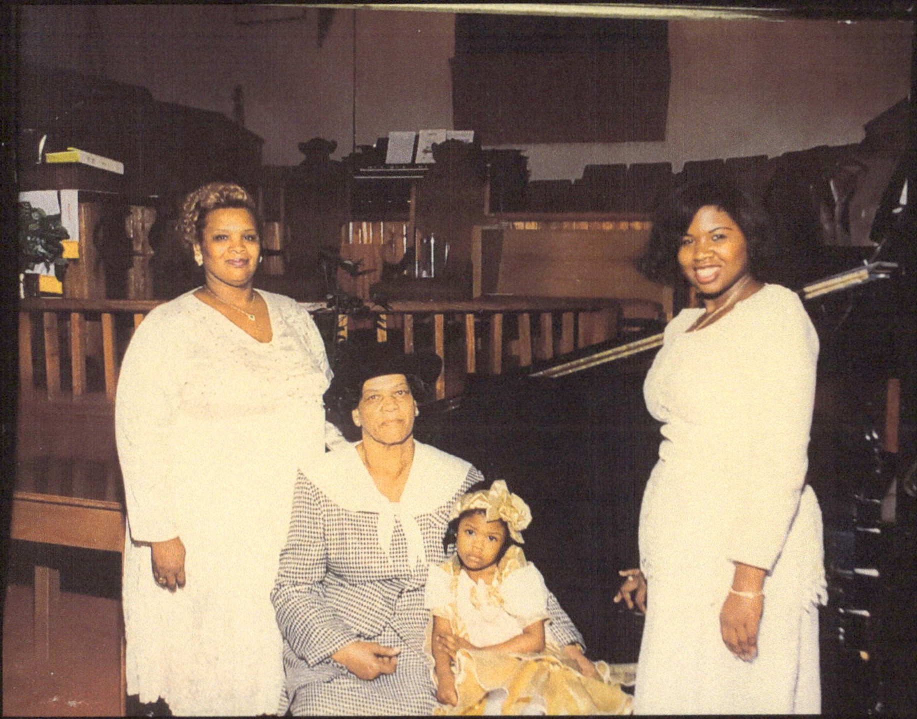

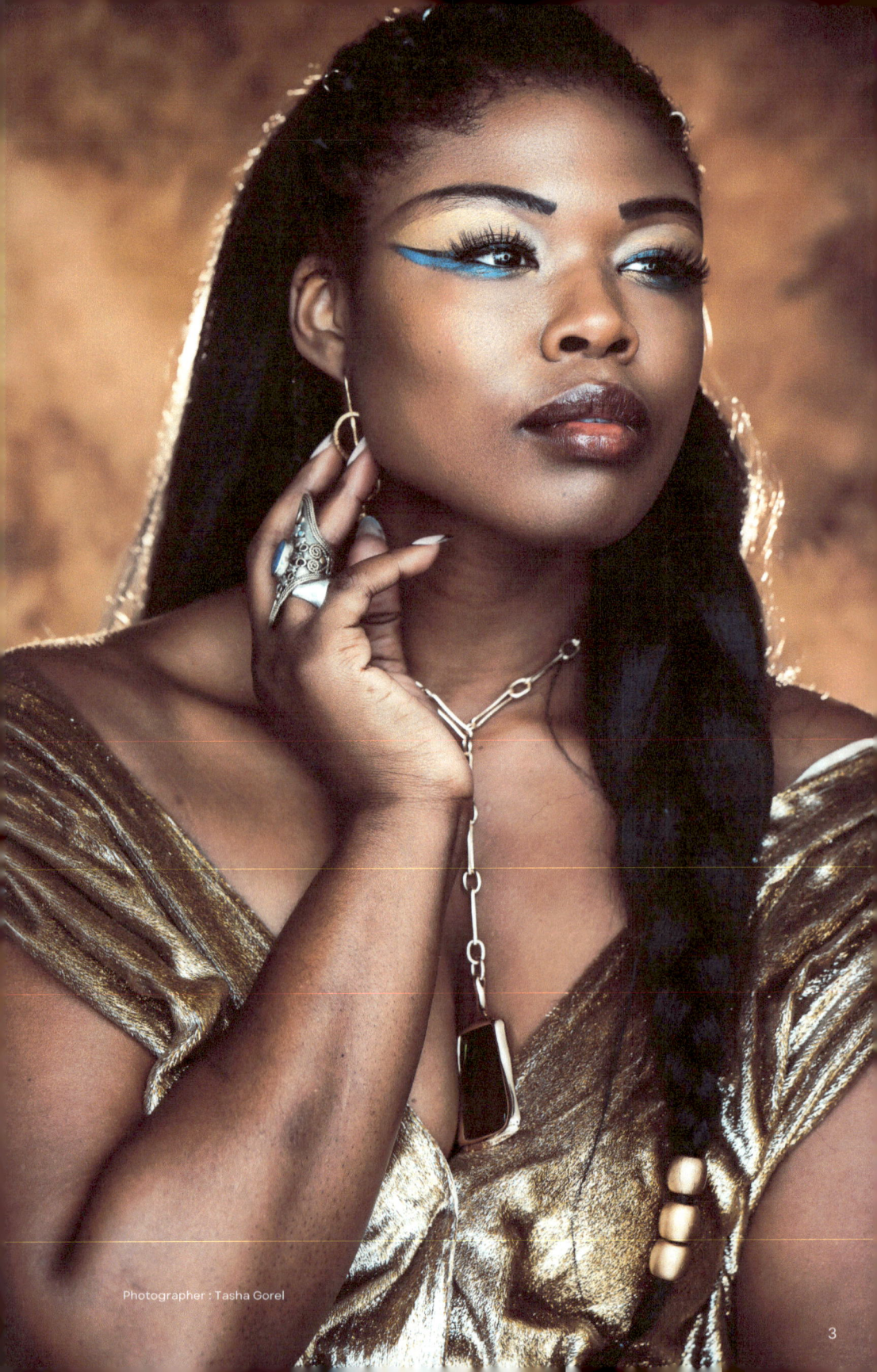

Photographer : Tasha Gorel

Cleopatra

ONCE A MILLENNIA IS THERE SUCH A
REMARKABLE WOMAN
CLEOPATRA
EGYPT CHILD OF PTOLEMY
THE LIVING ISIS
THE MOTHER GODDESS
FROM PAST TO PRESENT IS THE NAME OF
THIS DISTINGUISHED QUEEN SPOKEN
WITH DEFERENCE AND AWE
CLEOPATRA
RUTHLESS IN HER AMBITION
STRATEGIC IN HER LOVE
LET NOT LOVE LUST OR BLOOD STAND IN
THE WAY OF HER DESTINY
YOUR LIFE IS BUT A BOOKMARK IN THE
SAGA OF HER SUCCESS
ONCE SHE HAS YOU IN HER GRASP
MESMERIZED BY HER EMBRACE
HYPNOTIZED BY HER ALMOND EYES
SHE WILL LEAD YOU TO THE EDGE OF
THE UNIVERSE AND DARE YOU TO FLY
MAKE NO MISTAKE YOU ARE NOT THE
ONLY STAR IN HER UNIVERSE,
BUT SHE IS YOUR SUN MOON AND STARS
THE VENUS TO YOUR MARS
THANK THE GODS YOU ARE IN THE
PRESENCE OF
CLEOPATRA!

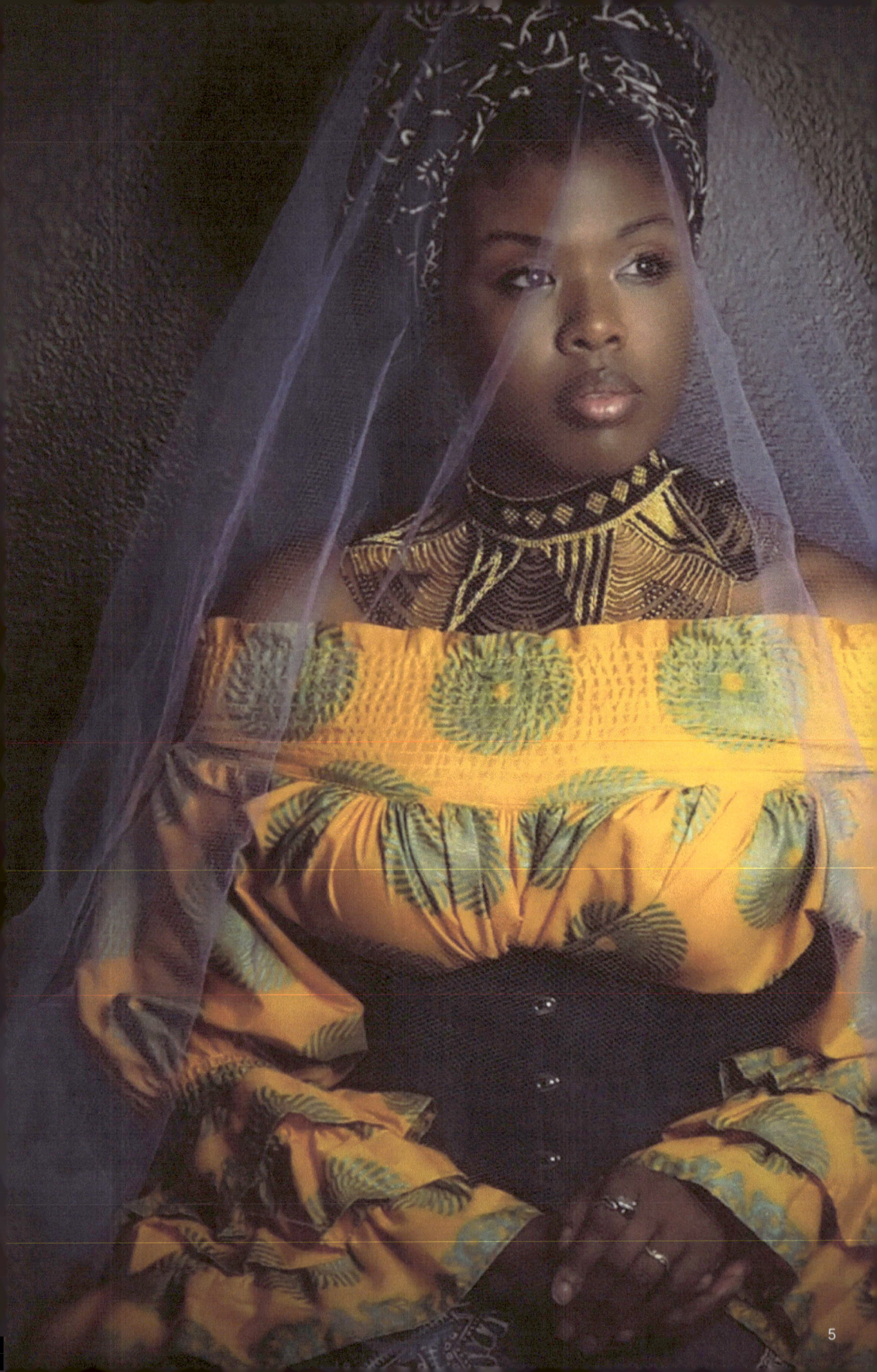

Divine

I AM NOT A WITCH I AM DIVINE.
WHAT YOU SEE BEFORE YOU
LONG LIMBS TIGHTLY COILED HAIR BROWN
SKIN ALMOND EYES, A LITTLE NOSE AND THICK
LIPS
THICK THIGHS, FULL BREASTS AND A
BOOTY. I CALL MY INHERITANCE.

THE LIGHT THAT RADIATES FROM WITHIN MY
SOUL
NESTLED WITHIN THIS DEEP COCOA
BOUNDS BETWEEN THE CURLS AND CURVES OF
THIS BRILLIANT BLACK GIRL
YOU FOUND YOURSELF INTOXICATED BY MY
EFFERVESCENT GLOW
WHICH OVERWHELMS YOUR SPIRIT
LIKE A CRAZY HIGH
NO
A BEAUTIFUL DREAM
NO
LIKE THE EMPTINESS OF A GAPING HOLE BEING
FILLED AND FULFILLED WITH A SUSTENANCE
NOT WHOLELY KNOWN
I KNOW YOU WANT ME
THAT'S CUTE, BUT I AM NOT SURE THAT YOU
ARE READY FOR THE RESPONSIBILITY OF THIS
LOVE
SORRY TO TELL YOU, BUT YOUR BURNING
DESIRE WON'T BE QUENCHED WITH JUST ONE
KISS FROM THESE LIPS
THE KISS WOULD JUST BRING YOU TO THE
PRECIPICE THE BEGINNING OF YOUR BLISS
WHERE DO I BEGIN?
LET START-
SKIN TO SKIN
WITH EVERY POINT OF CONNECTIVITY, THERE
IS A SPARK OF ELECTRICITY
THE RHYTHM OF OUR HEARTS DANCES IN STEP
READY FOR WHATEVER OUR BODIES SAY IS
NEXT

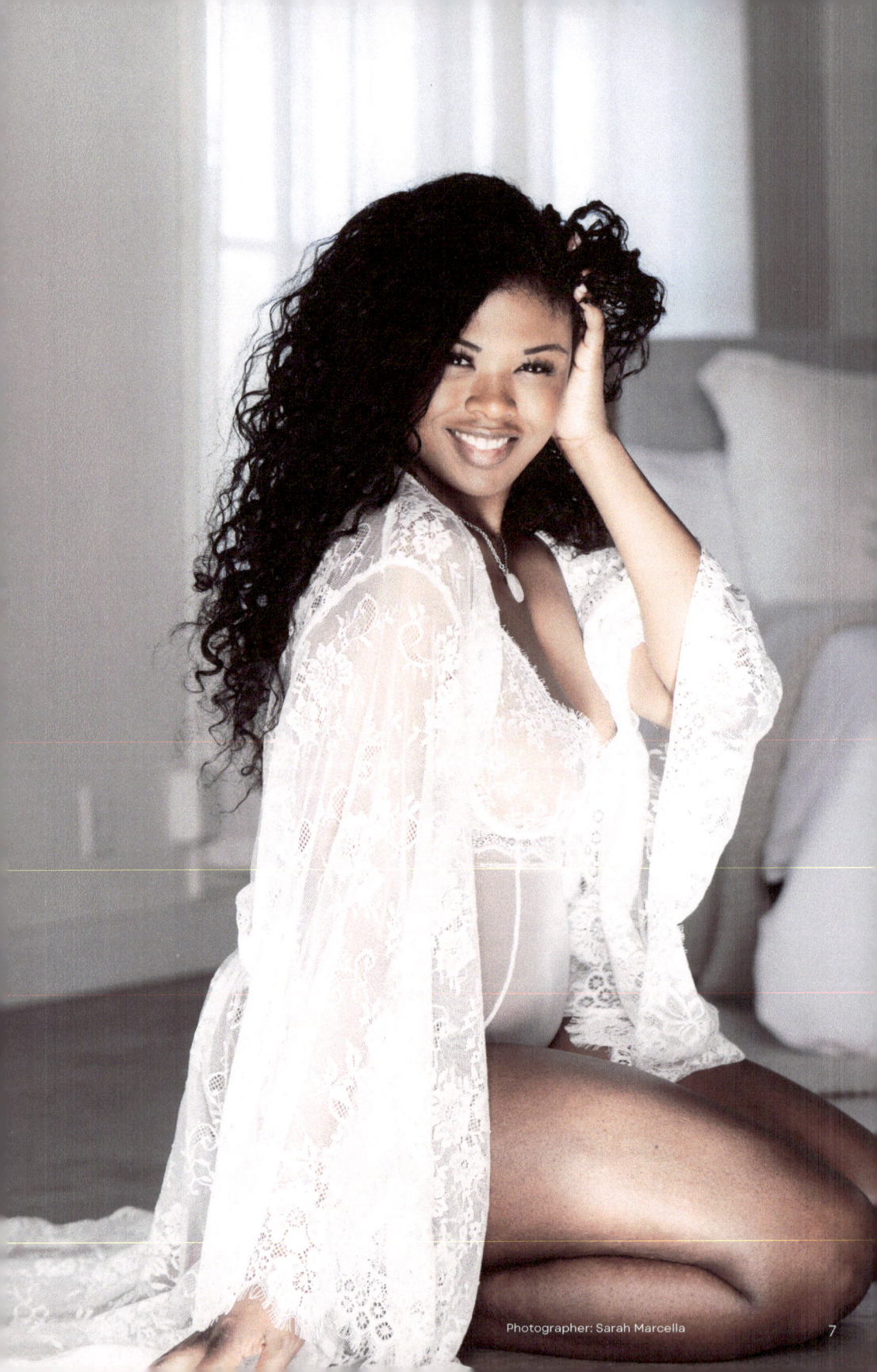

7

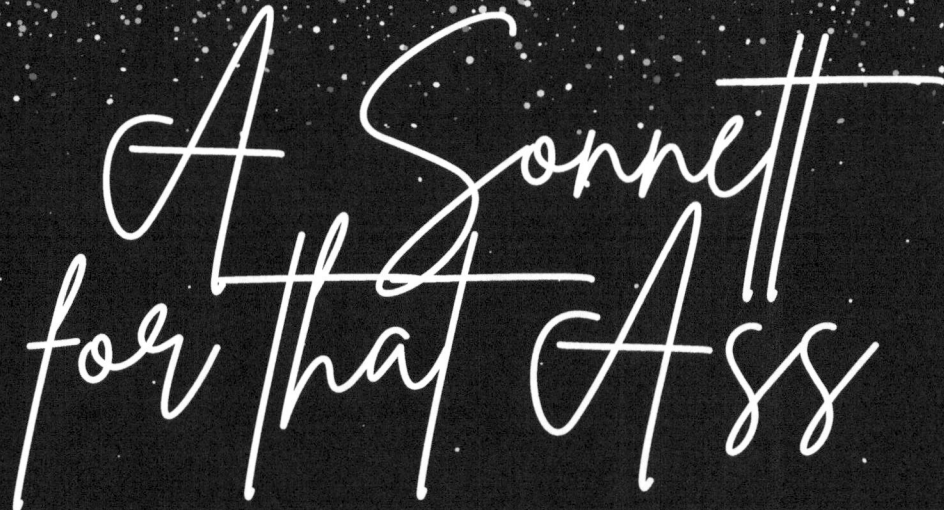

A Sonnett for that Ass

FROM ANCESTORS INHERITED
LANKY LIMBS, GRAVITY DEFYING COILS THAT
CROWN MY HEAD, DEEP ALMOND EYES
A LITTLE NOSE AND FULL LIPS
FROM WOMANHOOD, RATHER, MOTHERHOOD
BLOSSOMED BIG LEGS, FULL BREASTS, HIPS
AND OH MY GAWD LET'S NOT FORGET
MY INHERITANCE
THIS IS A LOVE LETTER TO MY BODY
THE VERY BODY THAT BROUGHT FORTH LIFE AND
GAVE OF ITSELF FOR MY BABIES' HEALTH
THIS IS MY REMINDER
CELEBRATE THE VIBRATIONS OF A BELLY LAUGH
AND APPRECIATE EVERY SWAY OF A GOOD DANCE
APPLAUD THE DIPS, CURVES AND SWERVES
YOUR BODY IS A SYMPHONY

HEY GIRL THIS IS A SONNET FOR THAT ASS
*SORRY MOM

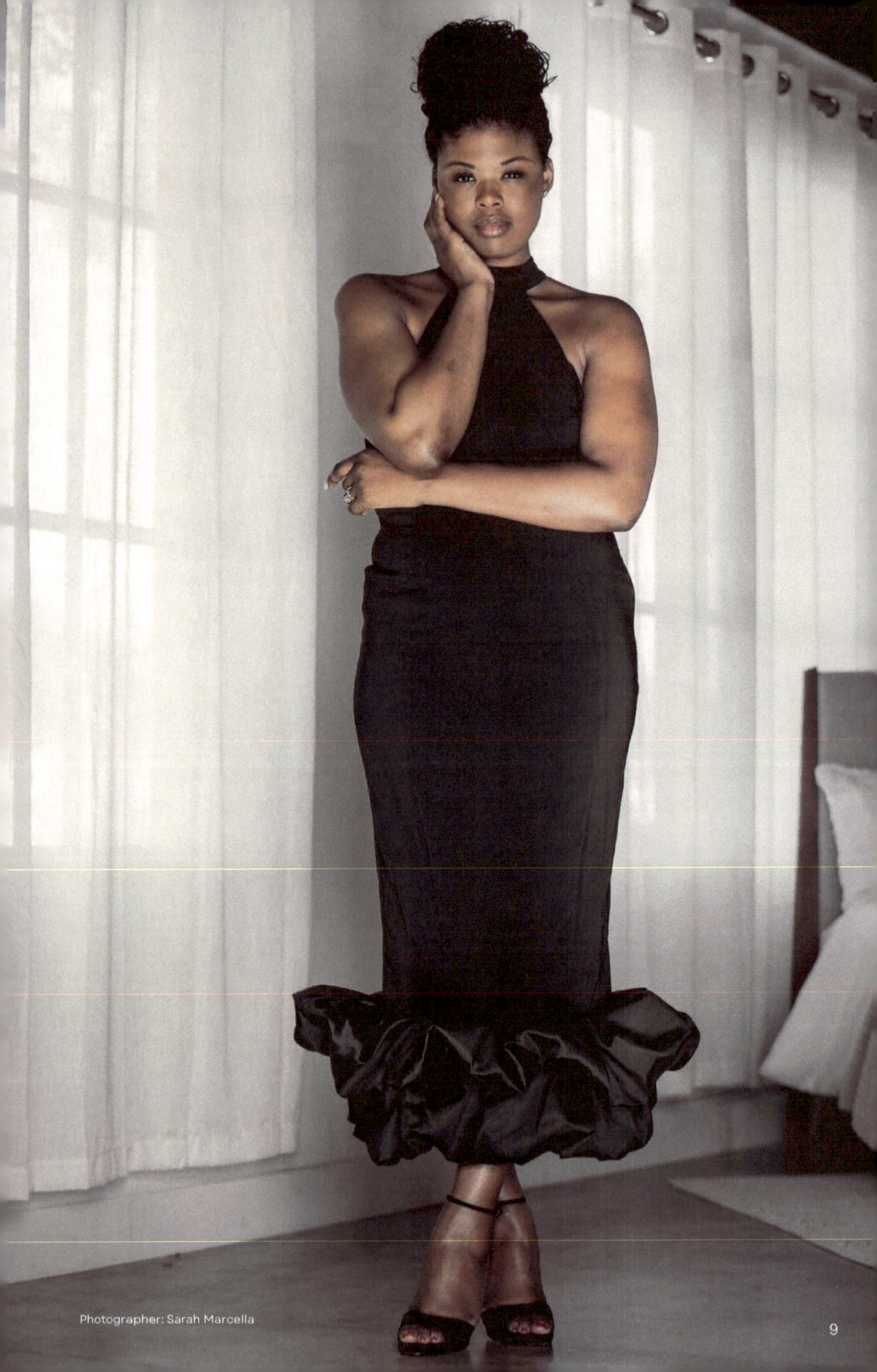

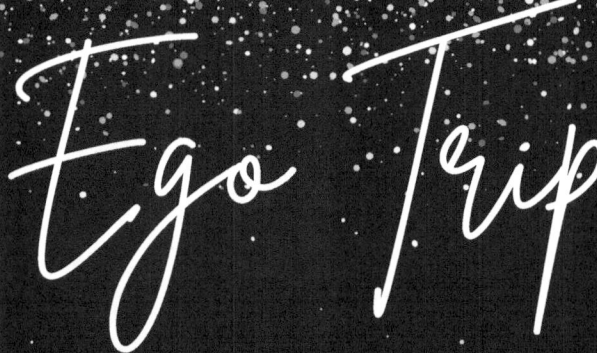

Ego Trip

THERE IS A SPARK OF DESTINY THAT FUELS ME
TO BE MORE THAN JUST AN EARTHLY THING
WHEN THE SUN PEAKS OUT OVER THE HORIZON
AND I RISE TO SHAKE OFF THE NIGHT
THE MOONBEAMS THAT CARESS ME IN MY SLEEP
FALL TO THE LAND TO CREATE HEALING
SPRINGS
I UNWRAP MY CURLS AND AS THEY SPRING TO
THE SKY THE FLY A WAYS TURN INTO BLACK
BUTTERFLIES
I AM A MOTHER A LOVER A DAUGHTER THE
DESCENDANT OF TRANSCENDENT WOMEN ON
WHICH WHOSE WINGS I FLY
I CARRY THE UNIVERSE IN MY WOMB
WHEN I GAVE BIRTH MY LABOR PAINS
ELECTRIFIED THE ATMOSPHERE AND ALL THE
TUNED SPHERES SANG FOR ME
HURRICANES IN SOUTHERN PLAINS HERALD THE
CROWNING OF THE LITTLE KING
MY FIRSTBORN THE LION KING CAME INTO THIS
WORLD WITH HIS FIST IN THE AIR
READY TO SHAKE IT UP AND TAKE HIS
BLESSINGS
HIS ROAR REACHES PAST THIS REALM AND
SHAKES THE ETHERS OF THE UNKNOWN
I WILL RAISE HIM TO STAND ON HIS
BIRTHRIGHT AND NEVER BEND UNDER THE
WEIGHT OF HIS OWN CROWN
FEROCIOUS WILL I BE IN THE PROTECTION OF
MY PRECIOUS PROGENY
MY SKIN IS MADE OF PURE GOLD
INTERNALLY ILLUMINATED BY STORIES UNTOLD
MY EGOTRIP IS A JOURNEY OF SELF-LOVE
SELF-APPRECIATION
APPRECIATION,
NOT JUST FOR THE MAGIC THAT I WAS BORN
WITH
BUT ALSO THE MAGIC THAT I CREATE

I HAVE DROPPED DIAMONDS AT YOUR
FEET WAITING FOR YOU TO NOTICE
ME
SO I AM
NOTICING MY DAMN SELF
MY DRIP IS FIRE
MY FLOW IS UNTOUCHABLE
I CAN SHOUT MY WORTH TO THE
ROOFTOPS
BUT IT'S TIME FOR THE TRUTH NOW
MY FAVORITE PASTIME IS DOUBT
IN MOMENTS WHEN I SHOULD SHINE
I SECOND-GUESS THIS LITTLE LIGHT
OF MINE
I TRIED AND TRIED TO FIT IN THE
CHORUS LINE
HOPING THAT ONE DAY YOU'LL GIVE
ME PERMISSION TO UNLEASH THIS
BOON OF MINE
I TOOK EXTRA STEPS FOR
RECOGNITION
BUT I HAVE TWO LEFT FEET WHEN IT
COMES TO THE SUPPRESSION OF MY
IPSEITY
I'M GOING TO SAY THAT AGAIN
IPSEITY, THAT SOMETHING THAT
MAKES ME UNMISTAKABLY ME
MY REVELATION CAME IN THE WEE
HOURS OF MY WALK OF SELF-HATE
THE WEIGHT OF MY NEED TO PLEASE
RENDERED ME INVISIBLE
ALL THAT WAS LEFT WAS A FLICKER
OF THAT LIGHT
I FOLLOWED THAT GLEAM TO THE
CENTER OF MY SOUL
AND I SAW IT
I SAW THE BRILLIANCE IN ME

WHEN GOD PUT TOGETHER THIS
COLLECTION OF CELLS
SHE STARTED WITH A PIECE OF
HERSELF
THE BINDING AGENT BEING THE BEST
OF WHAT MY ANCESTORS HAD TO
OFFER THE PEARLS THEY LEFT
BEHIND BECAME MY BACKBONE
THE SACRIFICES OF MY MOTHERS
BECAME THE LEGS I STAND ON
THE FORTITUDE OF MY FISTS ARE
BOLSTERED BY THE DREAMS OF MY
FATHERS
MY GENESIS OF SELF IS BUILT ON
THE BLOOD, SWEAT, AND TEARS OF
THE BLACK FOLKS BEFORE ME FOR
THE ADVANCEMENT OF OUR KIN
MY EVERY TRIUMPH IS A TRIBUTE TO
THE TRIBE BE THEY GREAT ARE
GARGANTUAN
THIS TIME MAYBE THE SHOWER OF
AFFIRMATIONS THAT I SHARE WITH
MYSELF WILL STICK TO MY BONES,
AND I WILL GRANT MYSELF THE
GRACE THAT I'M OWED.
I AM ENOUGH
I AM BEAUTIFUL
I AM BRILLIANT
I AM POWERFUL
I AM
I AM
I AM ALL THAT I AM MEANT TO BE
AND THEN SOME.

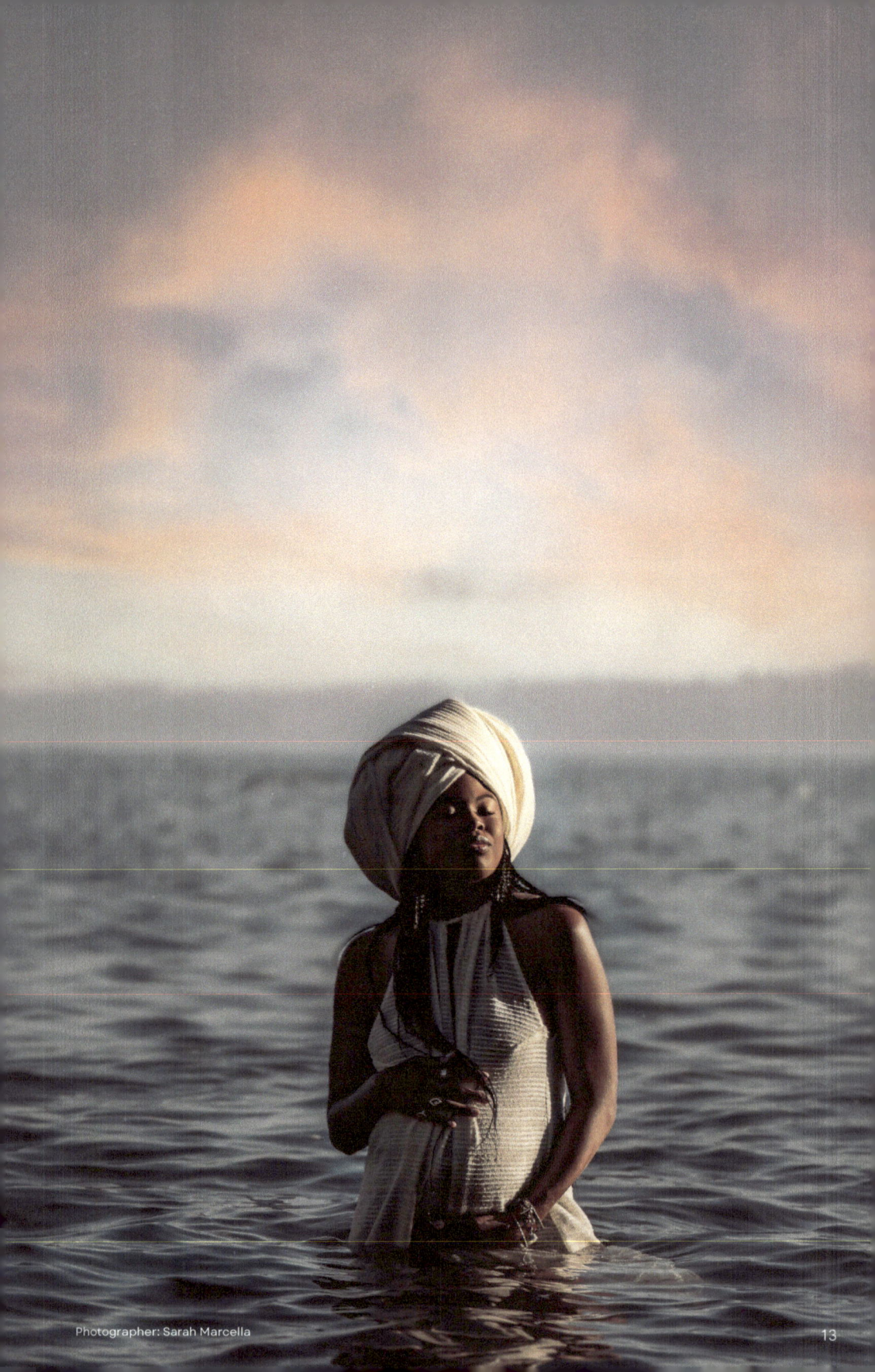

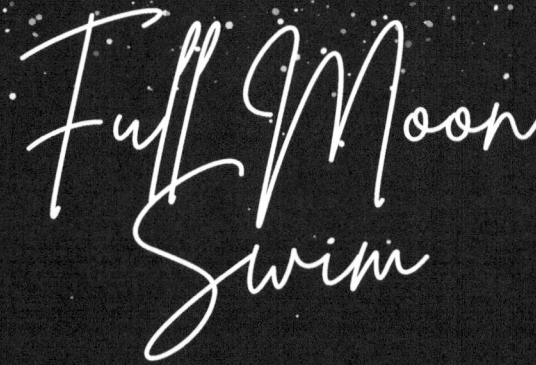

Full Moon Swim

DRIVEN BY THE RHYTHMS OF THE NIGHT SHE
RUNS AWAY TO ESCAPE THE HEAT
SHE DANCES
SWEAT POOLING AT HER FEET
DRESS CLINGING TO HER BODY
EVERY MUSCLE ENGAGED AS SHE ATTEMPTS
TO SPROUT WINGS AND FLY
THE WORLD AROUND HER BLURS AWAY INTO
A SWIRL OF COLORS
IF SHE STOPS THEN EXHAUSTION WOULD
MAKE A HOME IN THOSE WEARY BONES
BUT
TONIGHT SHE HAS NO TIME TO BE TIRED
WHEN THE FINAL BEAT HAS RESOLVED
SHE LOOKS UP AND FEELS THE CALL OF THE
MOON
ON THE EDGE OF THE OCEAN HYPNOTIZED BY
THE
INHALE AND CRASH
THE
EBB AND EXHALE
THE
SLAP AND FLOW OF THE OCEAN
SHE ALLOWS HER BARE BODY TO BE TAKEN
INTO THE EMBRACE OF
INYANGA
WRAPPED IN THE LIGHT OF THE MOON SHE
SHINES
IN THESE MOMENTS THE CHAOS OF THE
WORLD MELTS AWAY
AS THIS OCEANSIDE PARADISE GIVES BALM
TO HER SOUL

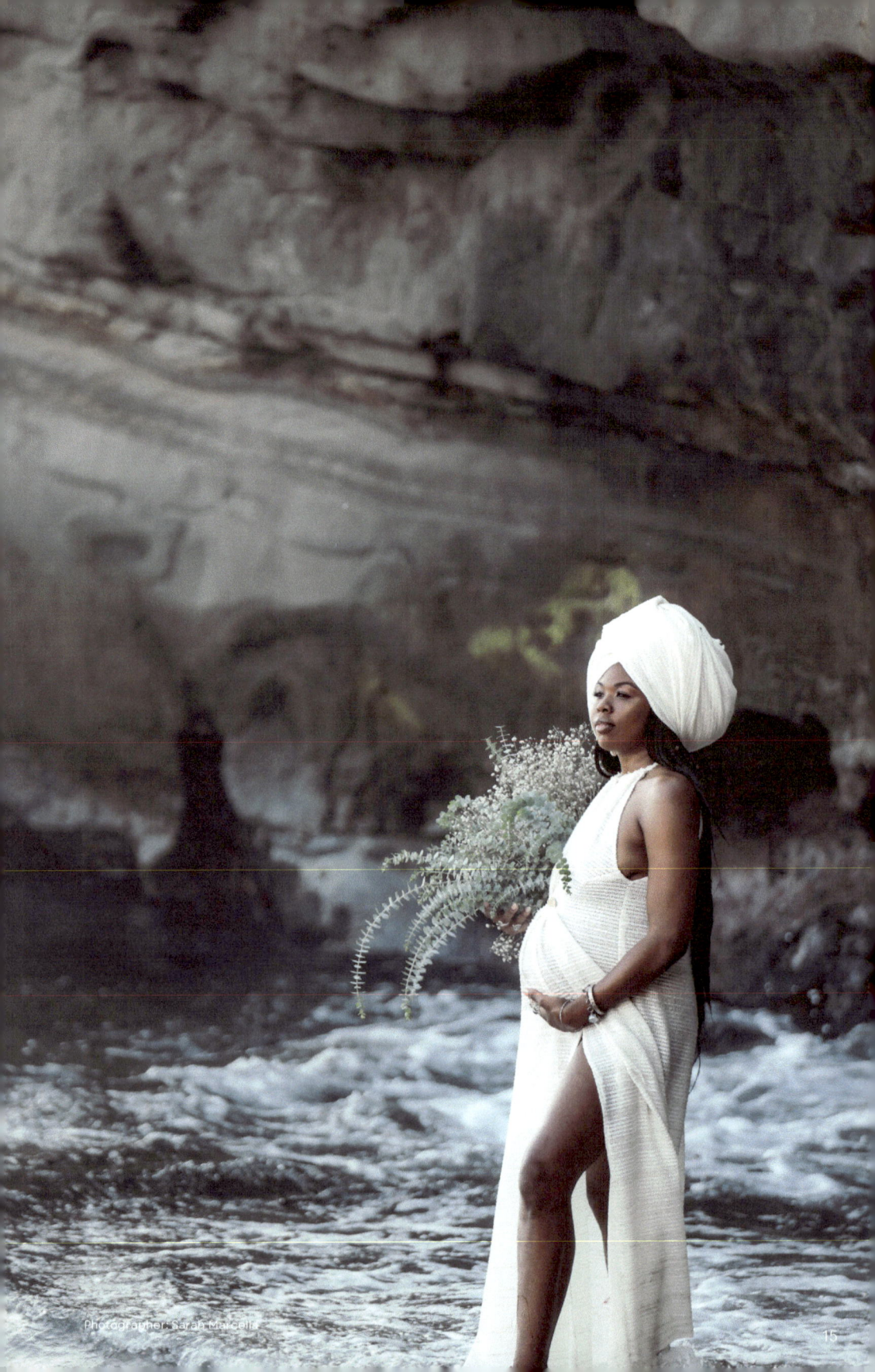

MY SPIRITUALITY IS
CULTURAL
MY FAITH IS UNFLAPPABLE
MY BOOGA BOOGAS RUN
DEEP AND ARE WASHED IN
THE BLOOD OF JESUS
I LOST MY TONGUE A LONG
TIME AGO BECAUSE I WAS
AFRAID
NOW I'VE FOUND MY VOICE
LIBERATED
&
FREE

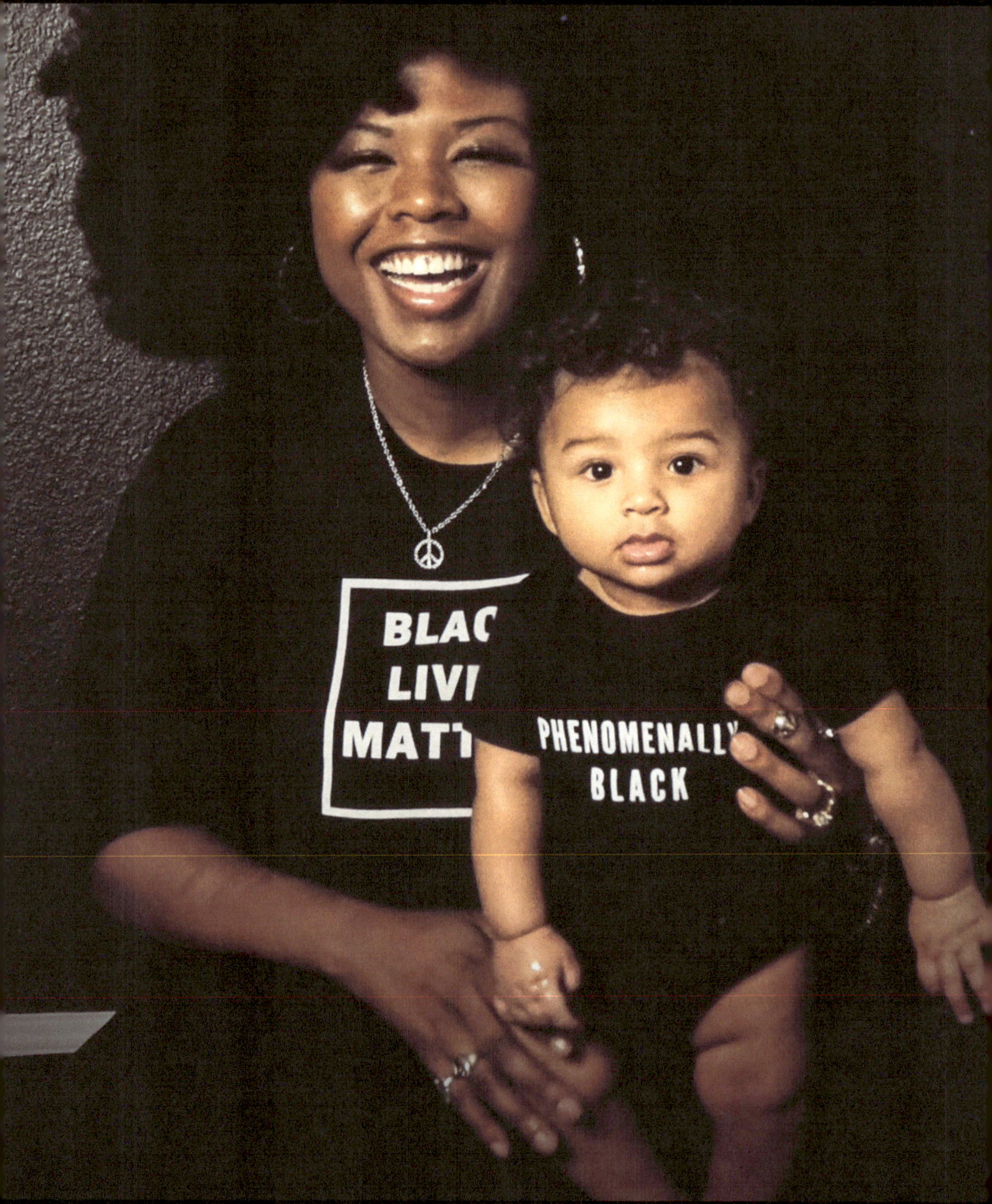
BLAC
LIVI
MATT
PHENOMENALLY
BLACK

Revolutionary

TO. DARE TO BE HAPPY IS A
REVOLUTIONARY ACT
WHETHER YOU ARE A DESCENDANT OF THE
ENSLAVED·OR IMMIGRANTS
ANTI-BLACKNESS IS A SICKNESS THAT THE
WORLD REFUSES TO LET GO OF
AND THROUGH ALL OF THE ADVERSITY
THROUGH ALL OF THE SYSTEMIC AND
BLATANT RACISM MEANT TO CRIPPLE US IN
EVERY SENSE OF THE WORD
WE REFUSE TO DISAPPEAR
WE REFUSE TO GIVE UP
WE REFUSE TO LET THE IGNORANCE OF
FOOLS HINDER OUR JOY
BLACK FOLKS HAVE DONE THE IMPOSSIBLE
WE HAVE SHAPED AMERICAN CULTURE AS
WE KNOW IT TODAY
WHILE FIGHTING FOR BASIC RIGHTS AND
RECOGNITION
BUT SOMEHOW WE CARVE OUT SPACE FOR
OURSELVES TO JUST SMILE
ON SUNDAY MORNINGS WHEN AUNTIE
THROWS HER HEAD BACK TO SAY
"THANK YOU"
ON SATURDAY NIGHTS SITTING ON THE
FRONT PORCH TALKING SHIT AND
LAUGHING LOUD
WHEN I WATCH MY SHOWS AND SEE
REPRESENTATION SO CLEARLY THAT IF YOU
KNOW THEN YOU KNOW
WHEN THE FAMILY COMES TOGETHER FOR A
MEAL THAT SEEMS TO STRETCH ON INTO
ETERNITY
FELLOWHIP IS HEALING
LAUGHTER IS MEDICINE
THE SMILE OF A BLACK CHILD IS MAGIC

18

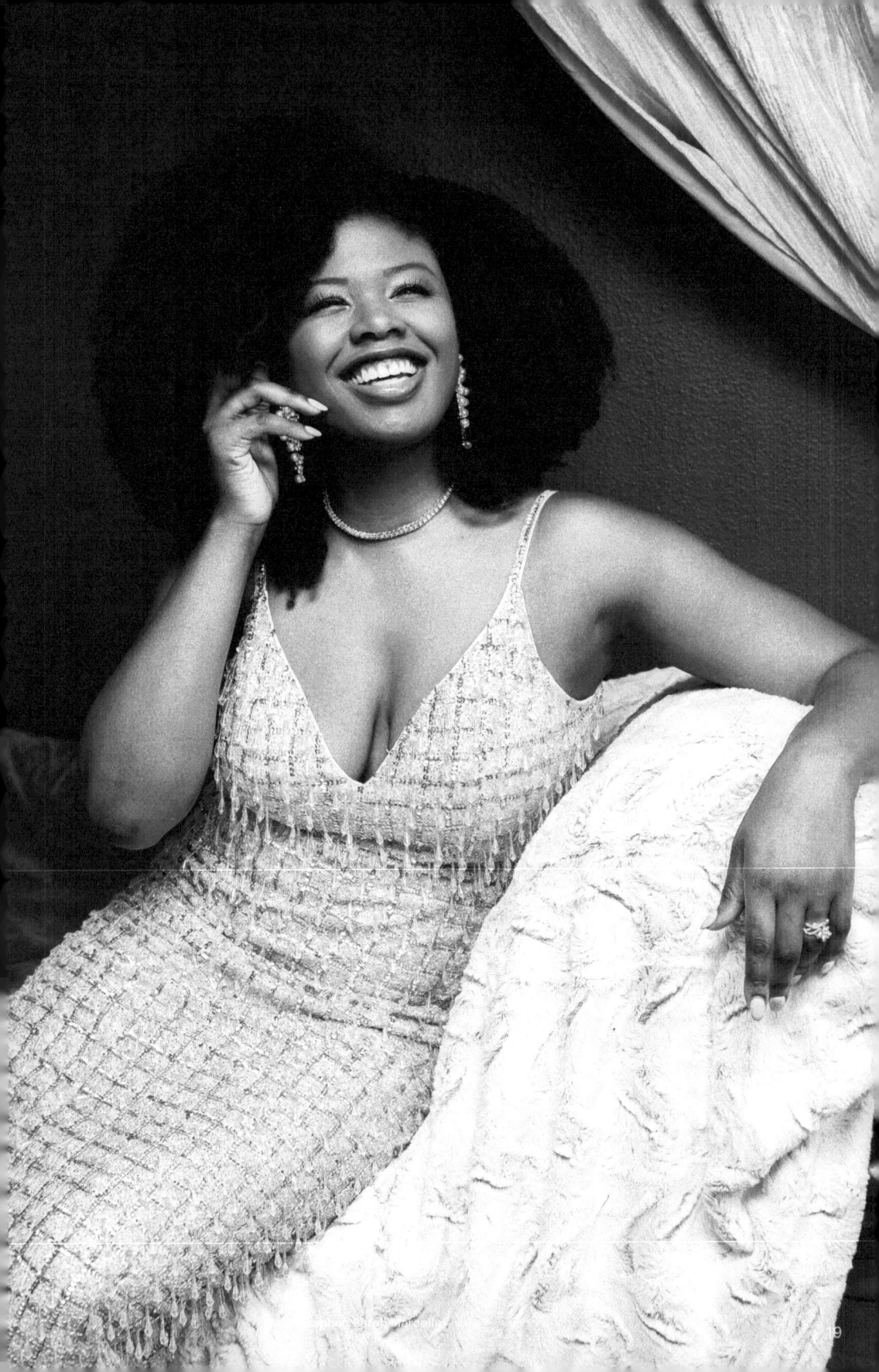

I DIDN'T KNOW I WASN'T THE
BEAUTY STANDARD
UNTIL
YOU TOLD ME SO
NOW
I AM THE STANDARD

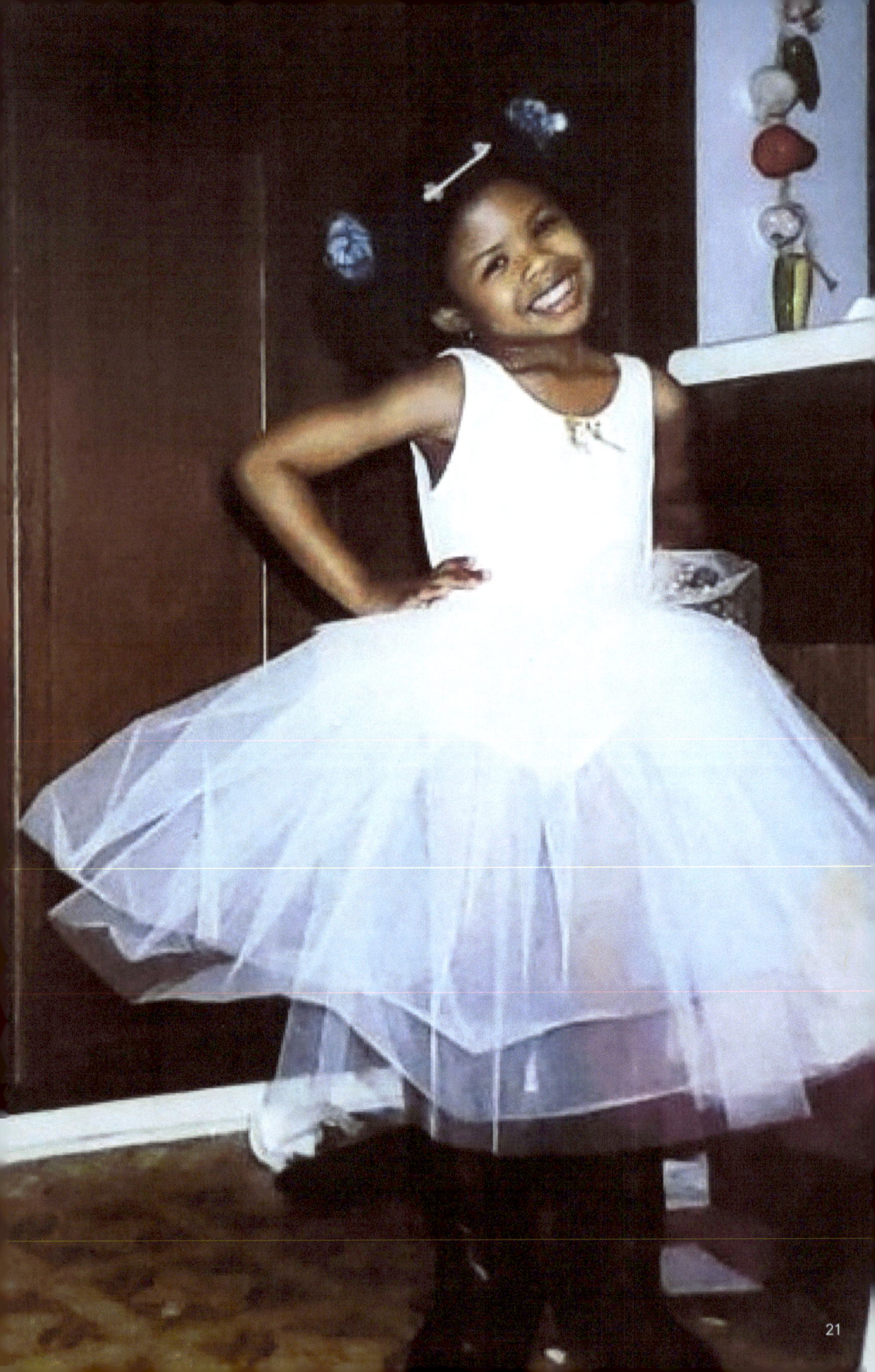

Growth

I AM BEING USHERED INTO A SEASON
OF SIGNIFICANCE
I AM UNCOMFORTABLE
MAKING UNCOMFORTABLE DECISIONS
BECAUSE MY UNIVERSE IS SHIFTING
AND IF I STAY STILL WILL MISS IT
MY BLESSING
THAT THING THAT I HAVE BEEN
TOILING OVER AND WORKING FOR
SHOUTING FROM THE ROOFTOP
THIS MOMENT IT MINE TO TAKE
SO THIS MOMENT OF DISCOMFORT IS
MOLDING
ITS ESSENTIAL
ITS NECESSARY
SOMETIMES YOU GOTTA SHED A LITTLE
SKIN
LET GO OF THAT PAIN YOU'VE BEEN
DRAGGING ALONG
STEP INTO YOUR PROMISE
WE GOT YOU

I AM GROWING

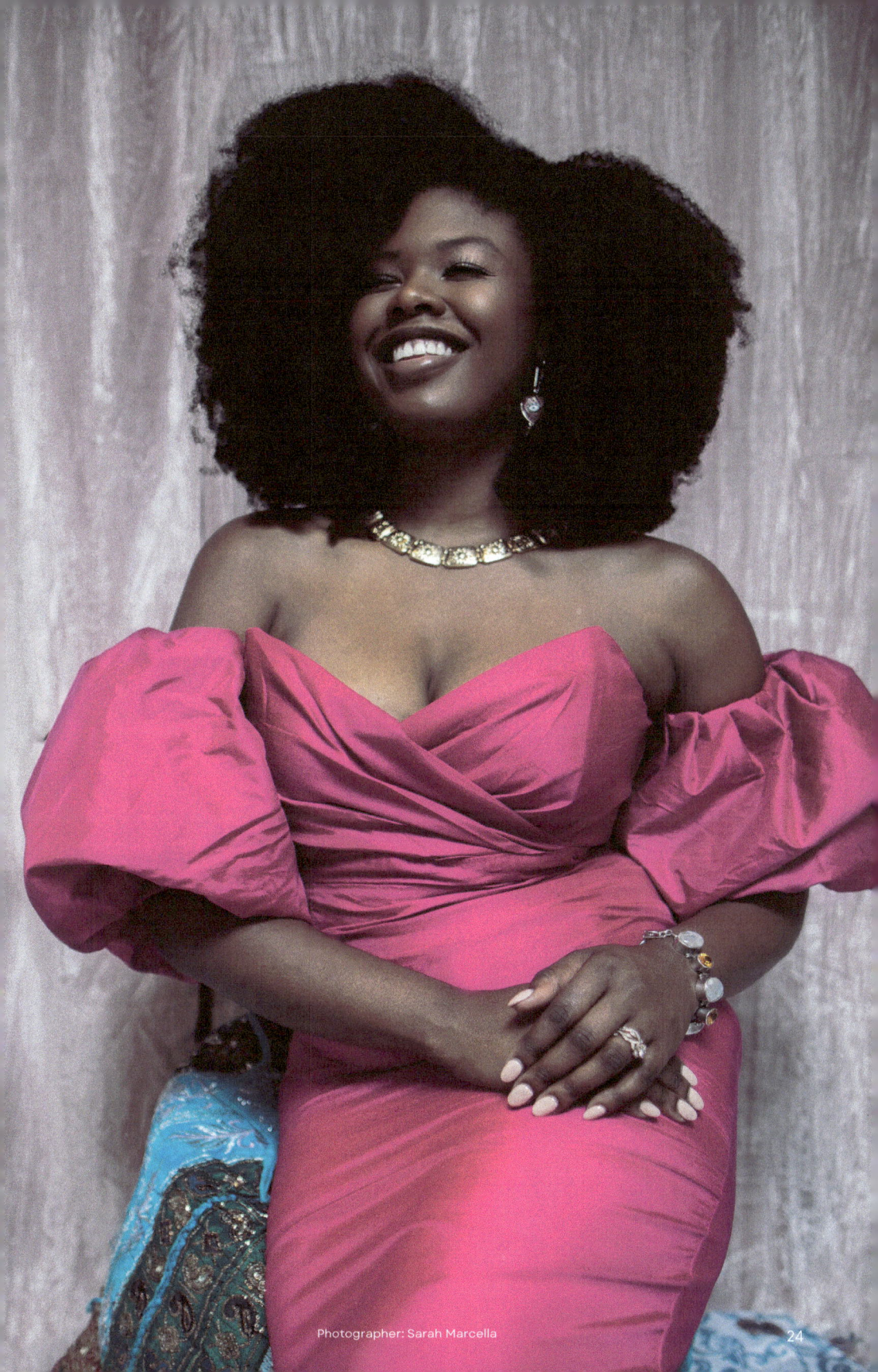

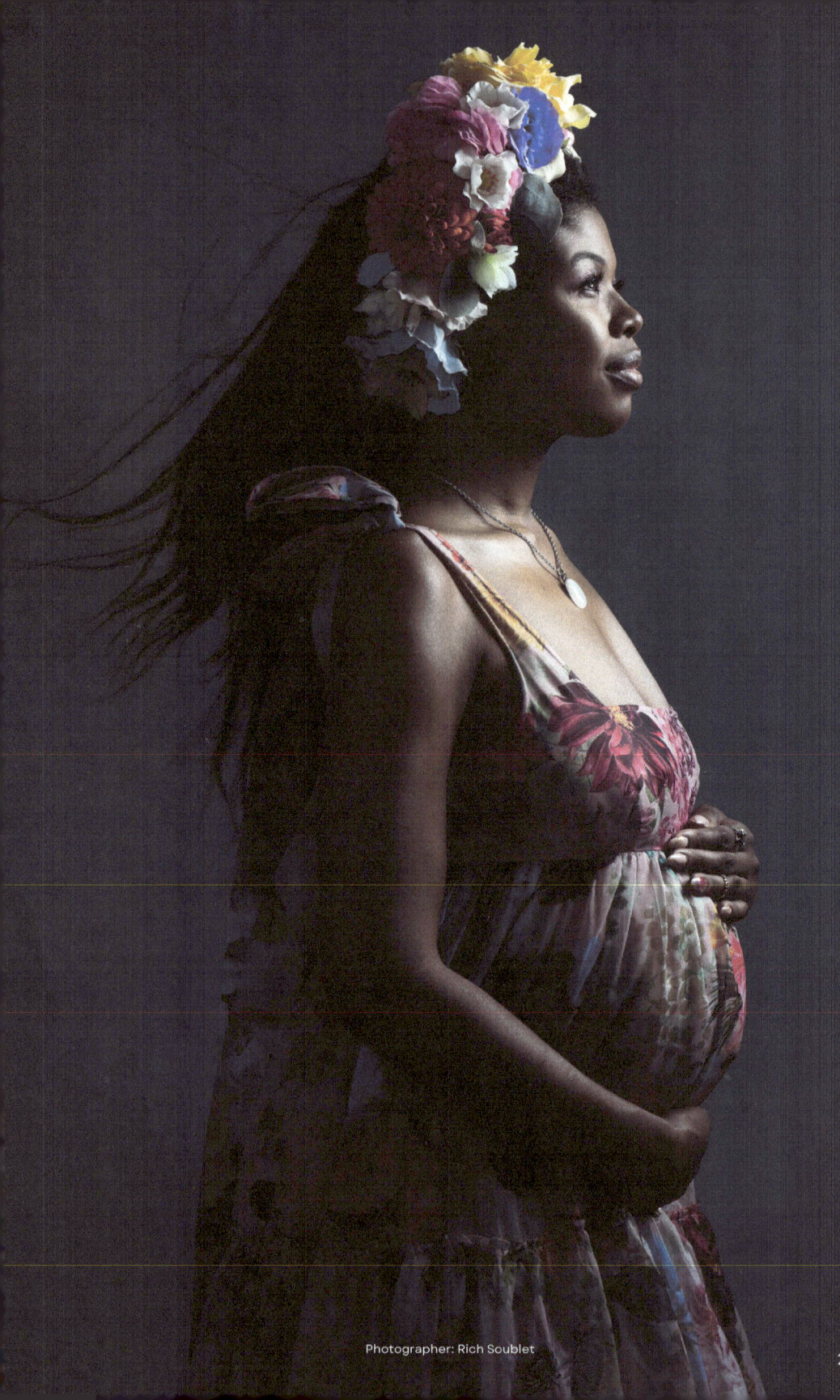

Photographer: Rich Soublet

Mamma

IN THE LIVING ROOM OF HER LITTLE BLUE
HOUSE SITS MOTHER.
SHE IS A WOMAN LIKE NO OTHER.
SHE SITS IN THE QUEEN'S CHAIR.
AN OLD WOODEN ROCKING CHAIR.
WHERE SHE HAS WATCHED ALL HER BABIES
GROW THROUGH HER LOVE AND CARE.
AT HER FEET SITS HER YOUNGEST BABY,
DAUGHTER AND ON HER SHOWER PEARLS OF
HER HISTORY.
THERE WAS A TIME WHEN WE WERE
CELEBRATED FOR OUR STRENGTH AND BEAUTY.
MEN WOULD GO OUT OF THEIR WAY JUST TO
HAVE A GLIMPSE OF OUR EBONY BEAUTY.
OTHER WOMEN WERE JEALOUS BECAUSE THEIR
MEN HAD DREAMS OF OUR TOUCH.
OUR CHILDREN GLORIOUS ANGELS THAT HELD
THE KEY TO THE FUTURE.
WE HAD TO BE ABOVE THE MUCK OUR GIFTS
HAD TO BE NURTURED.
FROM OUR WOMB WARRIORS, KINGS AND
QUEENS ARE BORN.
AND THE MAN THAT PROVED THAT HE
DESERVED OUR LOVE WOULD BE LOVED BETTER
THAN ANY OTHER MAN.
BUT IF HE WERE TO CONTAMINATE OUR LOVE
HE WOULD WISH THAT HE HAD NEVER SET EYES
ON US.
OUR WRATH IS AS FIERCE AS OUR LOVE.
THAT BEAUTIFUL EXISTENCE DIDN'T LAST
LONG.

GREED CAME IN THE NIGHT AND STOLE US FROM OUR HOMES.
TREATED US LIKE CATTLE AND TAUGHT US TO HATE EVERYTHING THAT MAKES US MAGNIFICENT.
LUST DREW THEM TO OUR BEDS AND CONCEIVED A HATE LEFT DEEP WITHIN OUR WOMB.
OUR CHILDREN USED TO CREATE A SYSTEM OF SUBORDINATION BASED ON COLOR.
THEY FOUGHT EACH OTHER WHEN THEY SHOULD HAVE CREATED AN ARMY.
WE HAVE FALLEN SO FAR...
BUT WITH EVERY GENERATION, WE GET CLOSER TO WHAT WE ARE SUPPOSED TO BE.
WE HAVE POURED ALL OF OUR JOYS, SORROWS, SETBACKS AND TRIUMPHS INTO YOU.

THE SPIRITS OF WISDOM, LOVE AND MOTHERHOOD SURROUND THE DAUGHTER.
FOR HER JOURNEY
THEY BESTOW THESE GIFTS:

WISDOM: LET HER SEE THE WORLD, AND LET HER BE SMART. SO THAT SHE CAN SEE DANGER BEFORE IT HAS THE CHANCE TO OVERTAKE HER.

LOVE: LET HER BE KIND, LOVING, CONFIDENT AND WILD. LET HER MAKE MANY MISTAKES.

MOTHER PRAYS, LORD LET HER BE HEALTHY AND THE REST WILL COME IN TIME.

THE DAUGHTER LOOKS UP AT HER MOTHERS WITH TEARS IN HER EYES...
"WHAT IF I'M NOT ENOUGH?"

WITH ALL THE PRIDE IN HER BODY
MOTHER STANDS FACE TO FACE WITH
DAUGHTER AND BETWEEN THEM
DANCES THE PAST, PRESENT AND
FUTURE.

THIS IS WHAT WE HAVE BEEN
PREPARING YOU FOR
YOU ARE A QUEEN CHILD!
THIS WORLD FULL OF IMITATION
AND CHEAP REPLICAS CANNOT
TAKE AWAY YOUR WORTH.

YOU ARE BLACK GOLD.

YOUR PLACE HAS BEEN FORGED IN
THE FIRES OF HISTORY
WHILE THEY ARE PAINTING THEIR
SKIN, BRAIDING THEIR HAIR AND
INJECTING THEIR BUTTS AND
CALLING YOU UGLY.

REMEMBER YOU WERE BORN
ENOUGH.

See me

ANXIETY IS KNOWING THAT YOUR VOICE CAN
MOVE MOUNTAINS, BUT EVERYONE ACTS LIKE
THEY CAN'T HEAR YOU
SO I SHOUT AND I WORK AND I SHOUT
SCHEME TILL I BURN OUT
BURN OUT IS
BEING HAUNTED BY YOUR AMBITION AND SO
DISCOURAGED THAT YOU FEEL PARALYZED IN
SPACE
SO I DROP EVERYTHING AND DISAPPEAR
AND YOU WONDER WHAT HAPPENED TO ME
BUT IF YOU JUST OPEN YOUR EYES AND SAW
THE STRIDES THAT I WAS MAKING OR
CLEARED YOUR EARS ENOUGH TO HEAR ME
SAY
DON'T GO THERE
LOOK HERE
SEE ME
MAYBE I WON'T DISAPPEAR

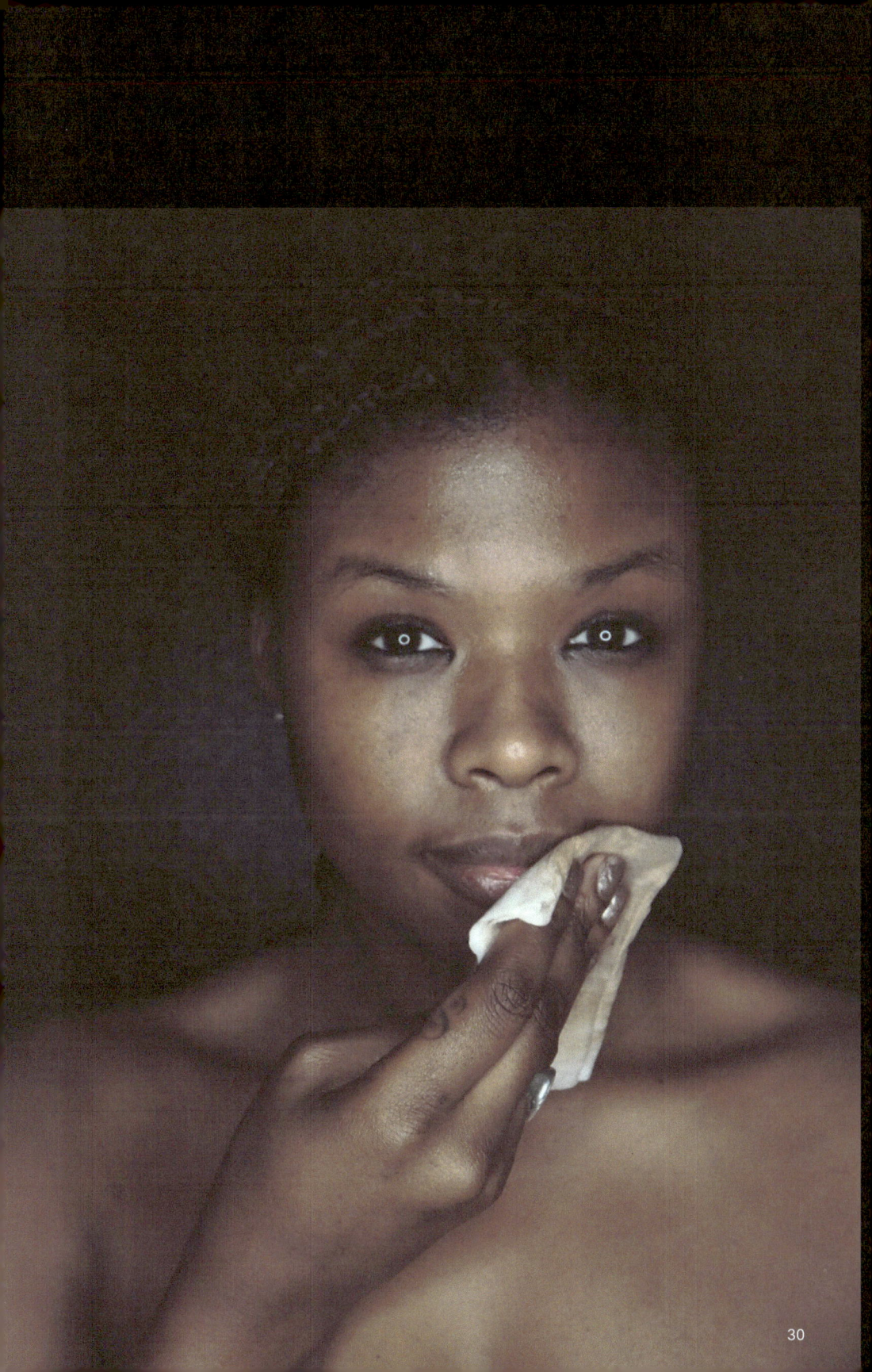

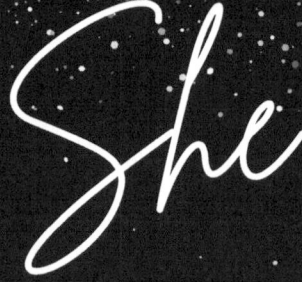

She

I KNOW WHAT YOU'VE HEARD ABOUT ME
STORIES FROM WOUNDED BOYS THAT
WANT TO REDUCE ME SIMPLE
SEDUCTRESS
I WANTED TO SURVIVE
I WANT ALL OR NOTHING
EVERYTHING THAT I'VE WORKED FOR
EVERYTHING THAT I DESERVE AND FOR
MY CHILDREN FOR HAVE THE THRONE
THAT I HAVE FOUGHT
THEIR BIRTHRIGHT
NO ONE WAS GOING TO ERASE ME.
ESPECIALLY NOT A MAN
NEVER MISTAKE ME FOR A DAMSEL
I FOUGHT THE WAY I MOVE BEST AND
WITH THE TOOLS HOWEVER SHARPEST IN
MY HANDS.
WHAT GOOD IS BEAUTY? IF YOU DON'T
KNOW HOW TO LEVERAGE IT.
WHAT GOOD IS INTELLIGENCE IF YOU
ARE AFRAID TO WIELD IT?
DOES THIS OFFEND YOU?
WOULD YOU PREFER ME TO BE A
LOVESICK KITTEN OR A MAD CAT IN
HEAT?
I LIVED BY MY RULES AND I DIE BY MY
WILL.
SAY WHAT YOU FEEL ABOUT ME BUT YOU
WILL NEVER FORGET ME.

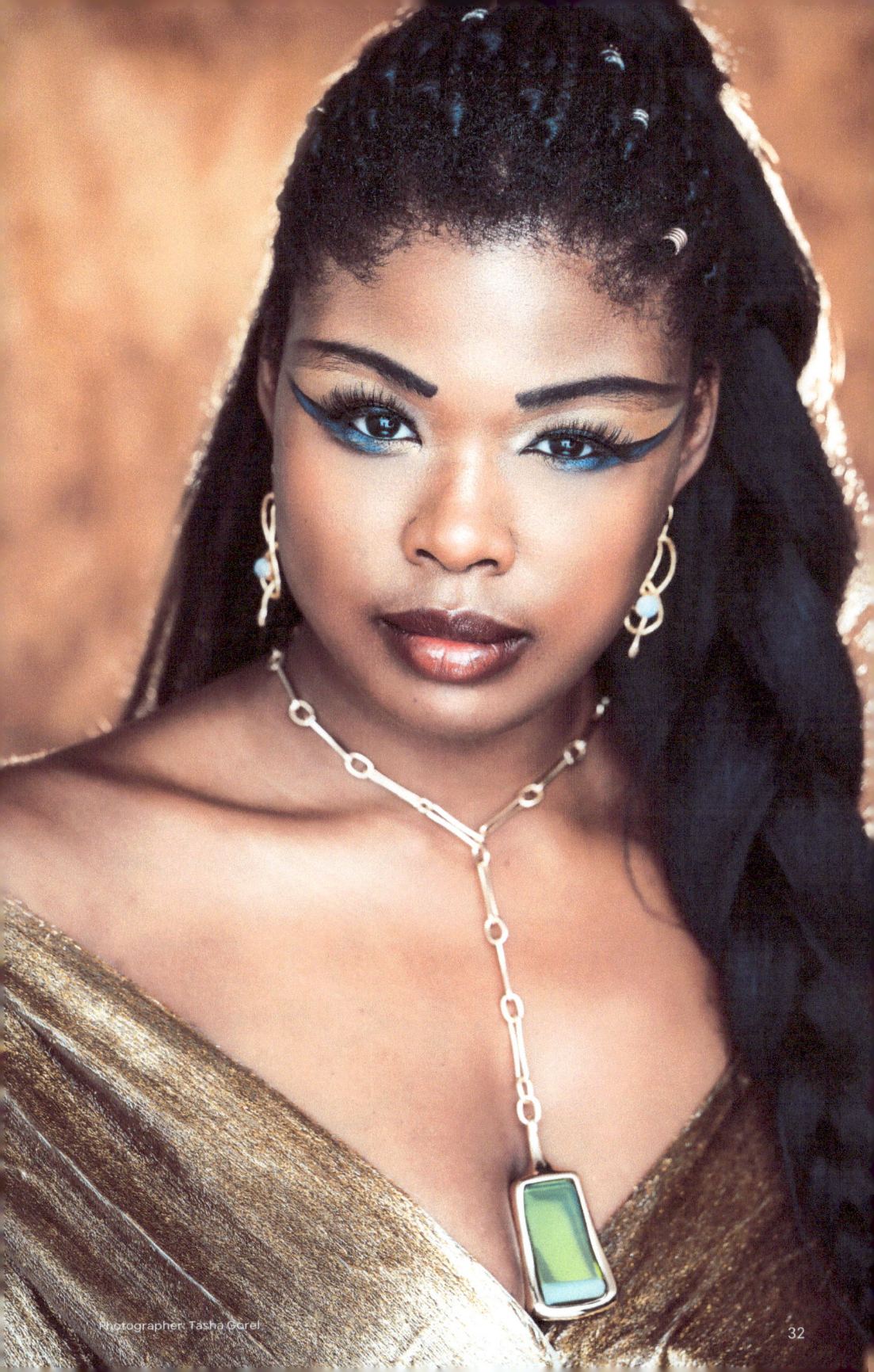

Photographer: Tasha Corel

32

To you,

I WANT TO BE YOUR MIRROR.
EVERY DAY YOU WAKE UP IN A
WORLD THAT CANNOT
COMPREHEND YOUR WORTH BUT
SOMEHOW YOU FIND A WAY TO
SMILE. YOU SPEND YOUR LIFE
SERVING OTHERS WATCHING
AND HEALING AND LOVING. YOU
GIVE WITHOUT ANY
EXPECTATION OF
RECIPROCATION. WE ALL FEEL
SAFE WITHIN THE FORTIFIED
WALLS OF YOUR HEART.

BUT
WITH ALL YOUR FIERCE
COMPASSION FOR EVERYONE
ELSE, YOU FORGET THAT YOU
ARE A MASTERPIECE.
LOOK IN MY EYES AND SEE A
TRUE REFLECTION OF YOU.

Joy Yvonne Jones

HOUSTON NATIVE, VETERAN'S WIFE, AND MOTHER OF TWO, JOY YVONNE JONES IS AN ACCREDITED ACTOR, POET, PLAYWRIGHT, MODEL, AND ENTREPRENEUR; WHO EMBODIES REVOLUTIONARY ART WITH EVERY PROJECT SHE IS A PART OF.

UPON GRADUATING FROM THE UNIVERSITY OF MINNESOTA IN THE GUTHRIE THEATRE BFA ACTOR TRAINING PROGRAM, SHE HAS GRACED FILM AND STAGE ACROSS THE COUNTRY. MOST NOTABLY RECEIVING THE SAN DIEGO CRITIC CIRCLE CRAIG NOEL AWARD FOR OUTSTANDING FEATURED PERFORMANCE IN A PLAY FOR HER PERFORMANCE OF SAARTJIE BAARTMAN IN VOYEURS DE VENUS AT MOXIE THEATRE.

HER STAGE CREDITS INCLUDE CAITLIN IN FERRYMAN (NEW VILLAGE ARTS), FRANCES IN MUD ROW (CYGNET THEATRE), CHERISE HOWARD IN FLEX (ACTORS THEATRE OF LOUISVILLE), JANE IN PRIDE AND PREJUDICE (CYGNET THEATRE), CLEOPATRA IN ANTONY AND CLEOPATRA (NEW MATCH COLLECTIVE), LADY MACBETH IN MACBETH (TEXAS SHAKESPEARE FESTIVAL).

IN 2020, SHE WROTE AND STARRED IN THE PLAY "ODE TO MY MOTHERS," WHICH WAS FEATURED IN THE OLD GLOBE THEATRE'S JUNETEENTH CELEBRATION. THIS POIGNANT AND PROVOCATIVE PIECE FOLLOWS THE STORY OF A YOUNG AFRICAN-AMERICAN WOMAN ON HER SELF-AWAKENING JOURNEY THROUGH THE LENS OF HER ANCESTRAL HERITAGE. JOY ALSO WROTE THE BOOK FOR GET ON BOARD, A PROTEST MUSICAL PREVIOUSLY PERFORMED AT LAJOLLA PLAYHOUSE'S WOW FEST (APRIL 2021) AND UCSD EPSTEIN AMPHITHEATER (JUNETEENTH 2023).

JOY IS A FOUNDING MEMBER AND PRESIDENT OF THE SAN DIEGO BLACK ARTIST COLLECTIVE. SHE SERVED AS ASSOCIATE ARTISTIC DIRECTOR OF NEW VILLAGE ARTS THEATRE IN SAN DIEGO.

SHE IS CURRENTLY WORKING ON THE REVOLUTION OF ART AT THE SPEED OF INSPIRATION WITH THE CREATION OF HER ONE WOMAN SHOW: CLEOPATRA, AND HER FUTURE SHORT FILM, A MONTH OF SUNDAYS. VISIT HER PATREON TO CONTRIBUTE AND BE INFORMED REGARDING THE DEBUT OF BOTH OF THESE WORKS OF ART.

YOU CAN LOOK FORWARD TO MANY EXPLORATIVE AND BOUNDARY-PUSHING WORKS FROM THE CREATIVE HURRICANE THAT IS JOY YVONNE JONES. YOU CAN FOLLOW HER ON INSTAGRAM, TIKTOK, AND FACEBOOK; @JOYYVONNEJONES OR VISIT HER WEBSITE: JOYYVONNEJONES.COM TO KNOW WHERE YOU CAN CATCH HER NEXT.

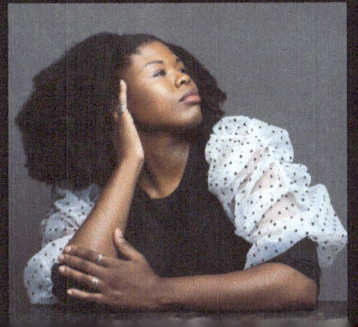

Photographer: Rich Soublet

Thank you!

NATASHA NIVAN PRODUCTIONS

SARAH MARCELLA PHOTOGRAPHY

RICH SOULET PHOTOGRAPHY
&
AUSTEN WHITE

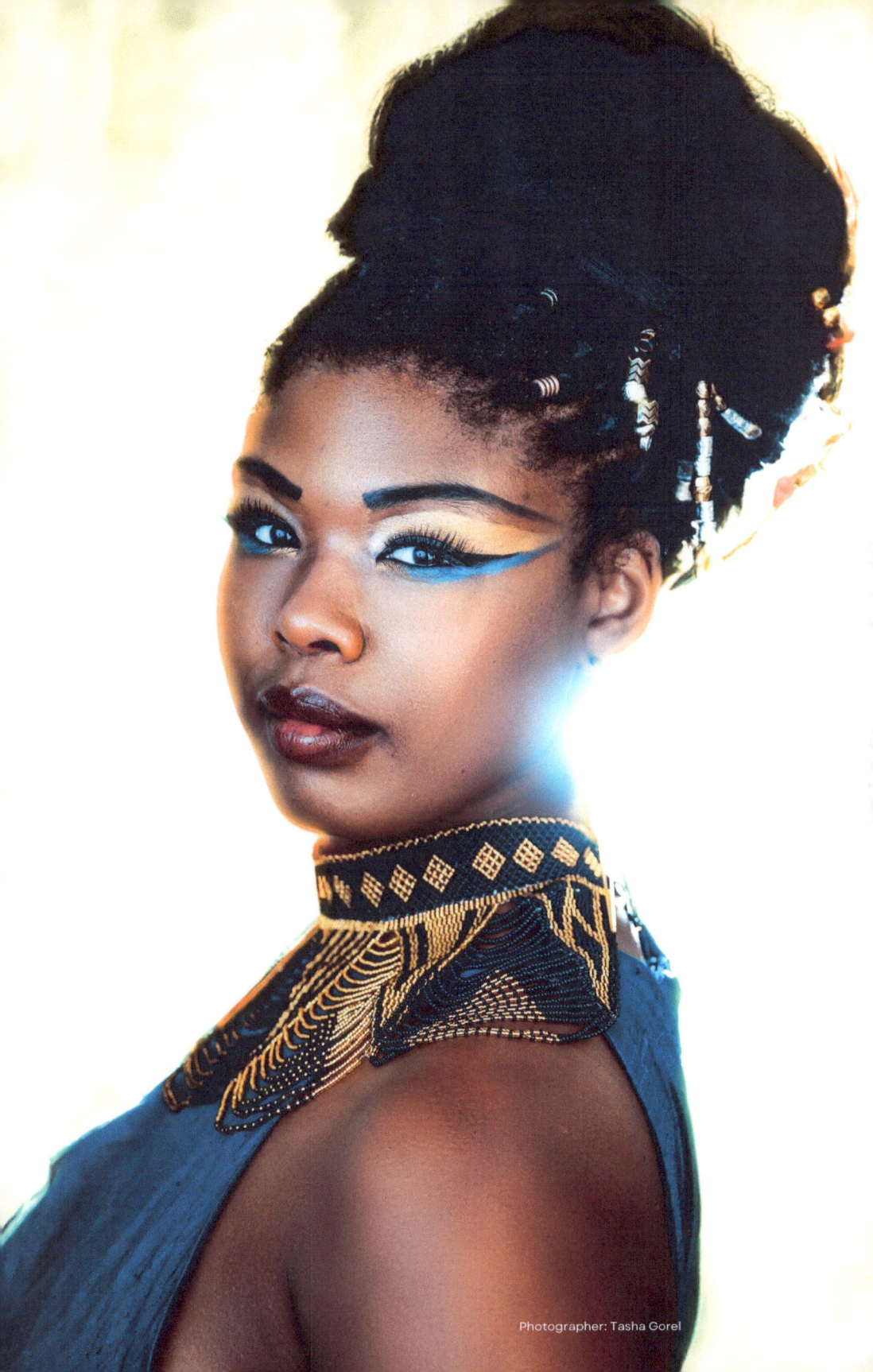